easy
ORIGAMI

A Step-by-Step Guide for Kids

by Mary Meinking and Chris Alexander

CAPSTONE PRESS
a capstone imprint

easy
ORIGAMI

A Step-by-Step Guide for Kids

by Mary Meinking
and Chris Alexander

3

TABLE OF CONTENTS

Chapter One — page 8
Easy Origami Projects

Chapter Two — page 34
Not-Quite-So-Easy Origami Projects

Chapter Three — page 60
Sort-of-Difficult Origami Projects

Chapter Four — page 86
Difficult Origami Projects

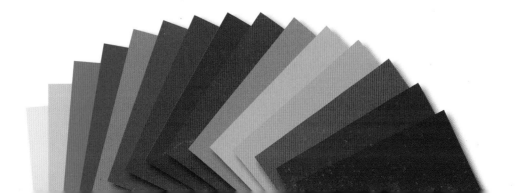

HOW TO USE THIS BOOK

Origami models are made with valley folds and mountain folds. All other folds are just combinations of these two basic folds.

Valley folds are represented by a dashed line. The paper is creased along the line as the top surface of the paper is folded against itself like a book.

Mountain folds are represented by a pink dashed and dotted line. The paper is creased along the line and folded behind.

Reverse folds are made by opening a pocket slightly and folding the model inside itself along existing creases.

Mark folds are light folds used to make reference creases for a later step. Ideally, a mark fold will not be seen in the finished model.

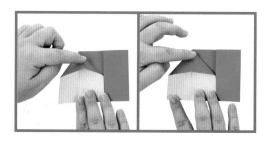

Squash folds are formed by lifting one edge of a pocket and reforming it so the spine gets flattened. The existing creases become new edges.

Outside reverse folds are two valley folds done at once. They are made by folding the model outside itself along existing creases.

Rabbit ear folds are formed by bringing two edges of a point together using existing creases. The new point is folded to one side.

FOLDING SYMBOLS

A crease from a previous step.	————————	Fold the paper in the direction of the arrow.	
A fold or edge hidden under another layer of paper; also used as an imaginary extension of an existing line.	· · · · · · · · · ·	Fold the paper and then unfold it.	
Turn the paper over or rotate it to a new position.		Fold the paper behind.	

MATERIALS

Before you begin, take some time to choose your paper. Traditional origami paper can be found at craft stores, on the Internet, and in some bookstores. It's usually colored on one side and white on the other. But you don't have to use special origami paper. Almost any kind of paper can be used for origami. Notebook paper, newspapers, dollar bills, and wrapping paper all can be folded into fun shapes.

Chapter One

easy
ORIGAMI
projects

EASY PROJECTS

Origami turns an ordinary piece of paper into a beautiful creation. Anyone can do origami with some paper and patience. Do valley folds, mountain folds, and squash folds sound strange to you? Keep reading. Soon, these folds will make perfect sense. Use them to make fun and easy models like paper cups and fortune-tellers. Even if you've never tried origami before, soon you'll be surprising family and friends with your new skills.

Where Did Origami Come From?

In AD 550, the Japanese were first introduced to papermaking. Before long, the Japanese began folding paper in familiar shapes to entertain young children. The word "origami" comes from the Japanese words *oru* meaning "to fold" and *kami* meaning "paper." Through traveling magic shows, origami was introduced to the world. The craft caught on, and people young and old alike have enjoyed making origami ever since.

HOW TO MAKE A SQUARE

Most origami models are made from square sheets of paper. If you don't have square origami paper, don't worry. It's easy to make your own from any size paper. Here's how:

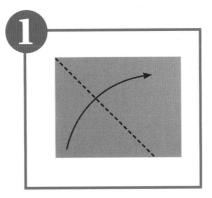

Fold the bottom left corner to the top edge.

Cut off the extra strip of paper.

A finished square.

PAPER CUP

Traditional Model

The next time you head for the drinking fountain at school, bring a cup. All you need is a sheet of paper and a few simple folds. But drink fast. This paper cup won't last long!

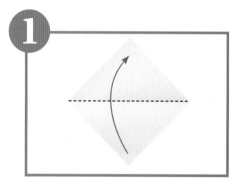

Start with the colored side down. Valley fold in half.

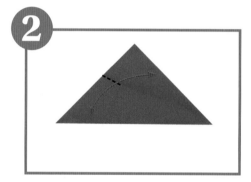

Mark fold the top right edge to the bottom edge and unfold.

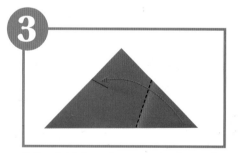

Valley fold the right corner to the mark made in step 2.

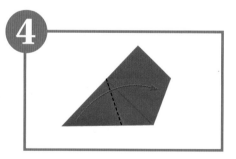

Valley fold the left corner to the right side.

5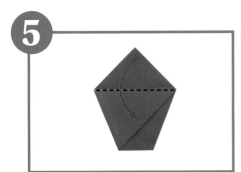

Valley fold the top layer.

6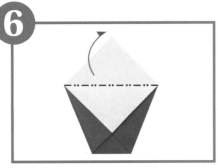

Mountain fold the remaining layer.

7

Finished paper cup.

Tea Time

These cups look like Asian teacups. Asian teacups come in different sizes. Small cups hold only one sip, while large bowl-sized cups are used in Japanese tea ceremonies. But unlike real teacups, paper cups should only be used for cold drinks.

SAMURAI HELMET

Traditional Model

Samurai warriors wore helmets called *kabuto* into battle. You could even make a *kabuto* that's large enough to wear. Just use a larger sheet of paper.

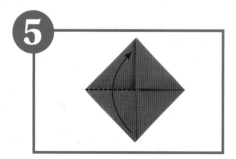

Start with the colored side down.
Valley fold in half.

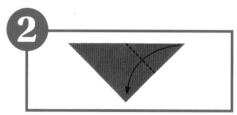

Valley fold the right corner to the bottom corner.

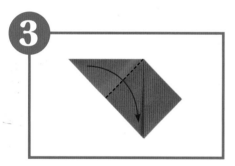

Repeat step 2 on the left side.

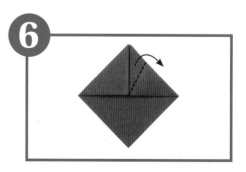

Valley fold the right flap to the top corner.

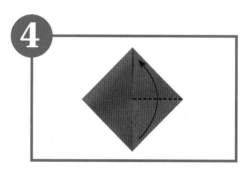

Repeat step 4 on the left side.

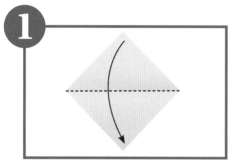

Valley fold the top tip to the right.

7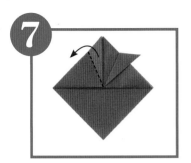

Repeat step 6 on the left side.

8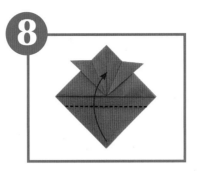

Valley fold the top layer.

9

Valley fold along the bottom edge of the helmet to create the brim.

10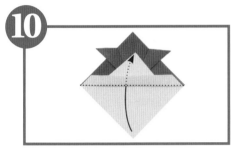

Valley fold the bottom corner into the helmet.

11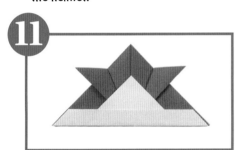

Finished samurai helmet.

Children's Day

In Japan, young children make and wear samurai helmets on Children's Day. This day is celebrated on May 5. Families fly streamers and fish-shaped windsocks. The streamers represent whips samurai leaders carried into battle.

HOUSE

Traditional Model

You can build your own mini home without bricks or nails. Use double-sided paper to create a colorful roof. The only thing left is to find a mini family to move in.

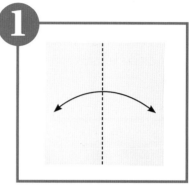

1

Start with the colored side down. Valley fold in half and unfold.

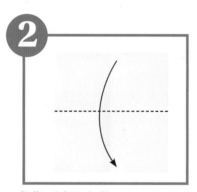

2

Valley fold in half.

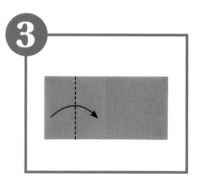

3

Valley fold the left side to the center crease.

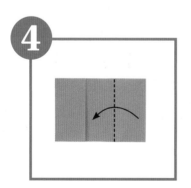

4

Repeat step 3 on the right side.

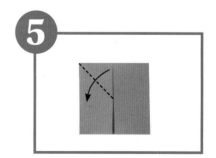

5

Valley fold the left side to the outside edge.

6

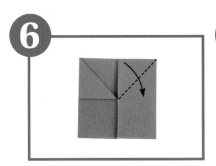

Repeat step 5 on the right side.

7

Squash fold the right side to create a roof.

8

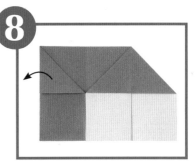

Repeat step 7 on the left side.

9

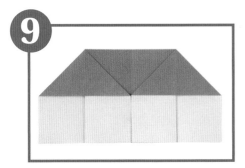

Finished house.

House Hints

Experiment in step 3 by changing the widths of the two roofs. Two narrow sides create barn silos or castle watch towers. Use smaller paper to make a mini doghouse or a birdhouse.

BANGER

Traditional Model

What's a party without a little noise? These bangers are a fun addition to any celebration. Make these noisemakers with ordinary notebook paper. Use a larger sheet of paper for a bigger bang.

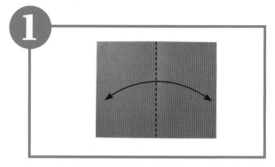

1 Start with a rectangular sheet of paper. Valley fold in half and unfold.

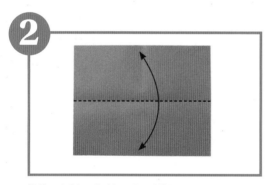

2 Valley fold in half and unfold.

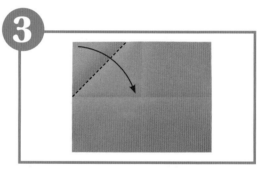

3 Valley fold to meet the crease made in step 2.

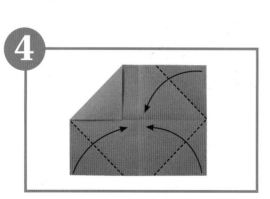

4 Repeat step 3 with the three remaining corners.

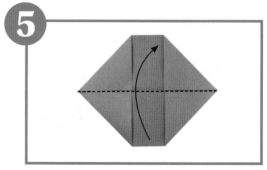

5 Valley fold in half.

6

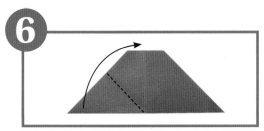

Valley fold the left side to the center crease.

7

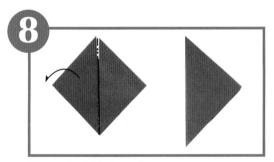

Repeat step 6 on the right side.

8

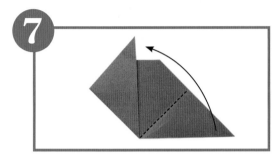

Mountain fold along the center crease.

9

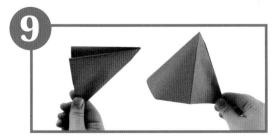

Finished banger.

How To Use

Hold the bottom two corners between your thumb and forefinger, with the single point facing your elbow. Quickly drop your arm down to create a "bang." Push the pocket back inside and repeat until your arm gets tired.

SPACESHIP

Based on a model by Makoto Yamaguchi

Check out a model that's out of this world. This spaceship flies across tables when you blow into the back. Make two and challenge a friend to a space race.

1

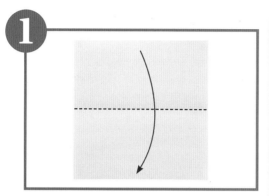

Start with the colored side down.
Valley fold in half.

2

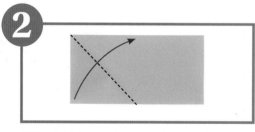

Valley fold the top layer to the top edge.

3

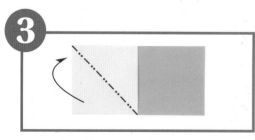

Mountain fold remaining layer.

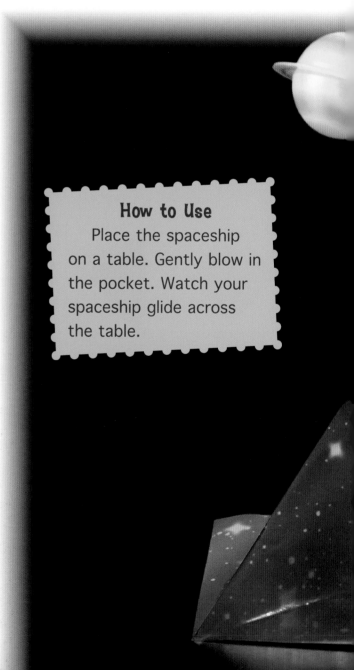

How to Use
Place the spaceship on a table. Gently blow in the pocket. Watch your spaceship glide across the table.

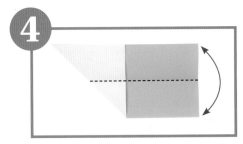

4 Mark fold in half and unfold.

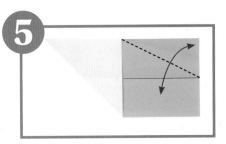

5 Valley fold from the triangle flap to the mark and unfold.

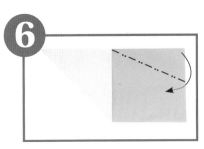

6 Reverse fold on the creases formed in step 5.

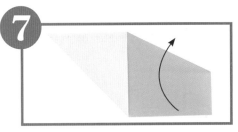

7 Lift the top flap.

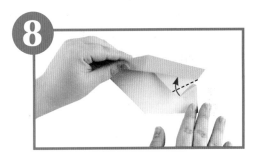

8 Valley fold along the roof. Close the flap.

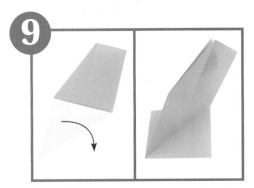

9 Unfold the creases made in steps 2 and 3 to create a base. Finished spaceship.

21

SPINNING TOP

Traditional Model

You'll need a big breath to make this top spin between your fingers. Use metallic paper for a shiny, strobe light effect.

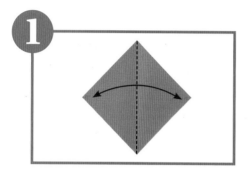

1 Start with the colored side up. Valley fold in half and unfold.

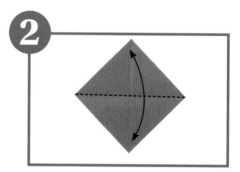

2 Valley fold in half and unfold.

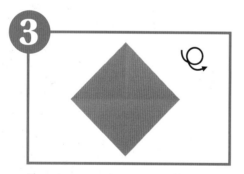

3 Turn the paper over and rotate.

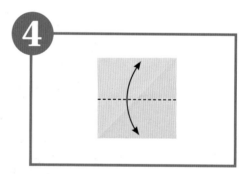

4 Valley fold in half and unfold.

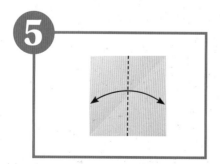

5 Valley fold in half and unfold.

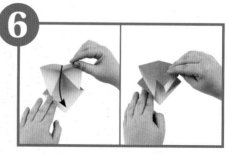

6 Squash fold.

7

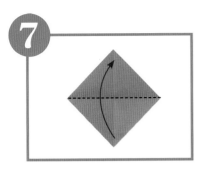

Valley fold the top layer.

8

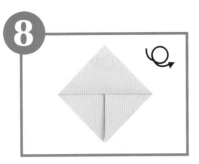

Turn the paper over and repeat step 7.

9

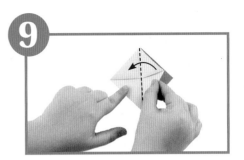

Valley fold the right side up.
Repeat behind.

10

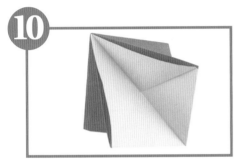

Finished spinning top.

How to Use
Loosely hold the tips between your fingers. Blow on the side and watch the top spin.

PYRAMID

Model designed by Mary Meinking

The Great Pyramid in Egypt was made using 2 million stone blocks. To make this miniature version, you only need a rectangular sheet of paper.

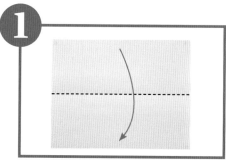

1

Start with a rectangular sheet of paper. Valley fold in half.

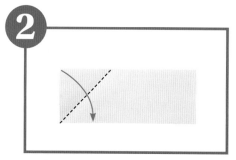

2

Mark fold the left side.

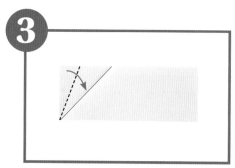

3

Valley fold to the mark made in step 2.

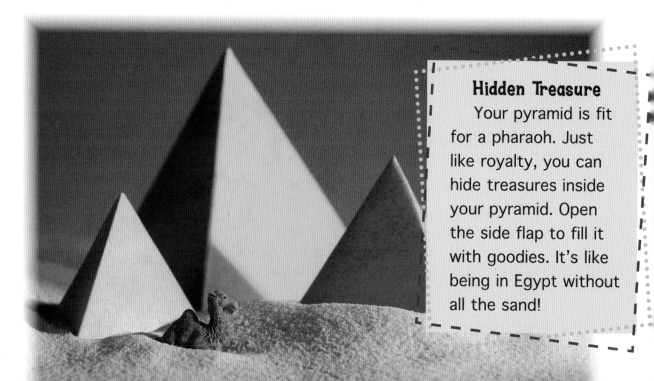

Hidden Treasure

Your pyramid is fit for a pharaoh. Just like royalty, you can hide treasures inside your pyramid. Open the side flap to fill it with goodies. It's like being in Egypt without all the sand!

4

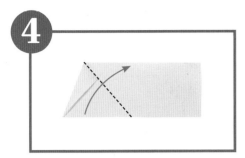

Valley fold to the top edge.

5

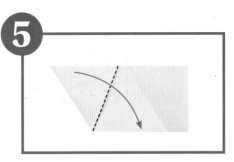

Valley fold to the bottom edge.

6

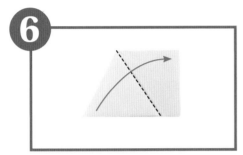

Valley fold to the top edge.

7

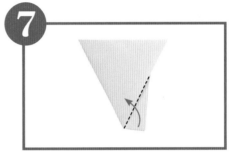

Valley fold the mini triangle.

8

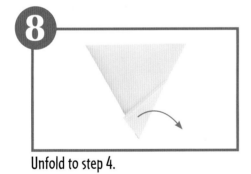

Unfold to step 4.

9

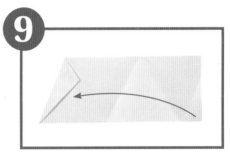

Tuck the corner into the pocket.

10

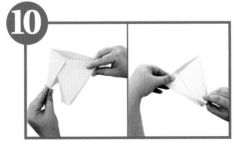

Push to form a snug edge on your pyramid.

11

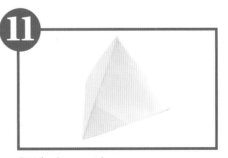

Finished pyramid.

HEART

Traditional Model

This heart will make a great Valentine's Day card for someone special. Instead of buying boxed valentines, you could make these for all your friends and family.

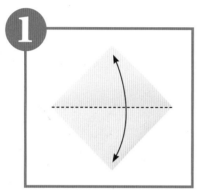

1 Start with the colored side down. Valley fold in half and unfold.

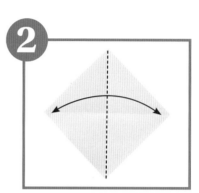

2 Valley fold in half and unfold.

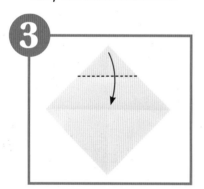

Valley fold to the center crease.

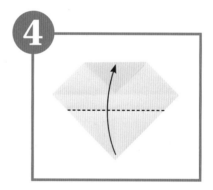

Valley fold to meet the top edge.

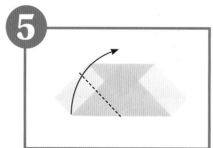

Valley fold the bottom edge to the center crease.

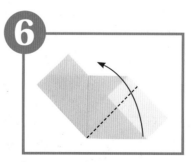

Repeat step 5 on the right side.

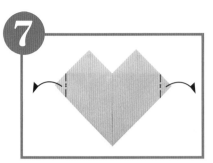

7

Mountain fold the corners.

8

Mountain fold the points.

9

Finished heart.

Be My Valentine

Friends and loved ones have exchanged Valentine's Day cards since the 1400s. Except for Christmas cards, Americans exchange more Valentines than any other type of card.

BUTTERFLY

Traditional Model

You can make a plain piece of paper come to life. This origami butterfly will flutter to the ground just like a real butterfly. The best part is you don't need a butterfly net to catch this one!

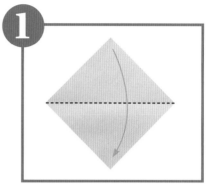

Start with the colored side down.
Valley fold the paper in half.

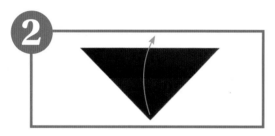

Valley fold past the top edge.

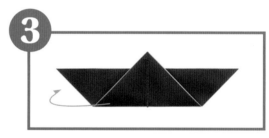

Mountain fold in half.

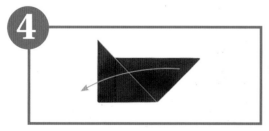

Valley fold the top layer to the left.

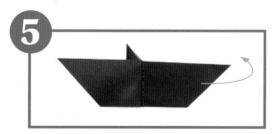

Mountain fold the right side.

6

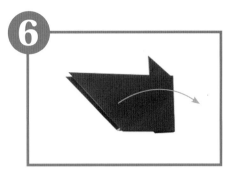

Lift up the two wings.

7

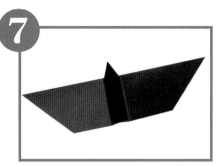

Finished butterfly.

How to Use
Point the triangle head of the butterfly forward and gently toss it in the air. Watch the butterfly flutter to the ground.

FORTUNE-TELLER

Traditional Origami

With this origami fortune-teller, your fortunes can be as serious or silly as you'd like. Gather a few friends and get ready to see what the future holds.

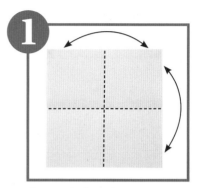

Start with the colored side down.
Valley fold in half both ways and unfold.

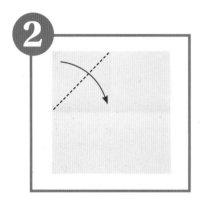

Valley fold the corner to the center.

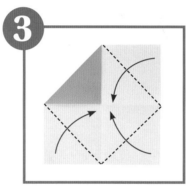

Repeat step 2 with remaining corners.

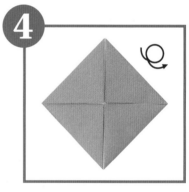

Turn the paper over and rotate.

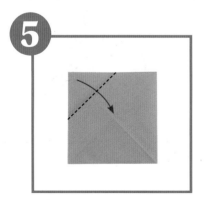

Valley fold the corner to the center.

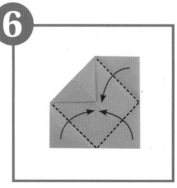

Repeat step 5 with the remaining corners.

Valley fold in half.

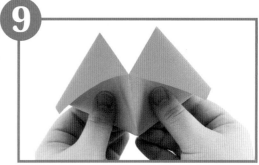

8 Push your thumbs and index fingers into each of the four bottom pockets.

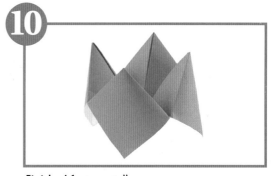

9 Push up and to the center until the points meet and the pockets open.

10 Finished fortune-teller.

How to Use

Flatten to step 7. Write different numbers or words on each of the eight small triangles. Lift the flaps to write fortunes on each of the eight triangles. Turn over. Write different colors on each of the four squares. Refold to step 9. Have a friend pick a color. With your fingers inside the pockets, open and close once for every letter. Then have your friend pick a number. Lift that flap to see your friend's fortune.

FUN FACTS

- The artist/inventor Leonardo da Vinci was one of the first famous paper folders. He folded parchment into flying machines to understand the principles of flight. Many consider da Vinci the father of paper airplanes.

- Akira Yoshizawa was a master origami folder. He created more than 50,000 origami models. He also created the international origami folding symbols of arrows and lines that folders still use today.

- Origami is used for all types of advertising, including TV commercials. Origami has been found in commercials for cars, cat food, pizza, chocolate, and fast food restaurants.

- The magician Harry Houdini amazed audiences when he folded paper into unusual shapes. In 1922, he wrote a book called *Houdini's Paper Magic*, which included four origami models. Turning ordinary paper into an extraordinary model is, after all, a magical process.

- You don't need paper to fold origami. On cruise ships, towels are commonly used to fold lobsters, elephants, and other fun shapes. Room attendants leave these animals in passengers' rooms. When passengers return from dinner, they are often surprised to see these origami animals on their beds.

WHAT'S NEXT. . .

After completing the models in this section, you're ready to test your skills. The next part of this book is Not-Quite-So-Easy Origami.

You'll learn how to make models like a trapdoor envelope, a hopping frog, and a flapping crane. These projects use the same folds you have already learned. They have more steps, but with a little practice you'll master them in no time.

not-quite-
so-easy
ORIGAMI
projects

NOT-QUITE-SO-EASY PROJECTS

Ordinary paper has a secret identity just waiting to come out. With just a few folds, you can turn plain paper into something wonderful. Will it turn into an airplane, a cicada, or an envelope? Use your imagination to make just about anything out of paper.

Some origami models may seem tricky at first glance. But don't get scared off by many steps or difficult folds. Take your time to learn each step. If you get stuck, don't give up. Just back up and try again. With a little practice, you'll soon become an expert.

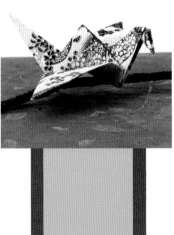

Meet Mary Meinking

Mary Meinking made the easy and not-quite-so-easy projects in this book. Mary grew up enjoying arts and crafts with her mother and two younger sisters. She took art classes where she drew and painted. Mary decided to turn her hobby into a profession. She studied art at the University of Kansas. Mary shares her love for arts and crafts with her two children. Together they enjoy folding origami and paper airplanes. She currently lives in Spirit Lake, Iowa.

TRAPDOOR ENVELOPE

Based on a model by Jeremy Shafer

Pass out party invitations in this envelope, and you're sure to get a response. Have your friends pull on the tab. They'll be surprised to see the envelope burst open and the contents spill out.

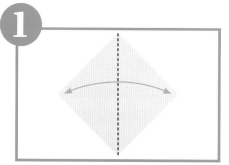

Start with the colored side down.
Valley fold in half and unfold.

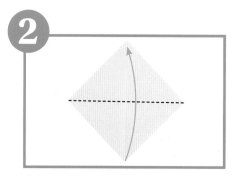

Valley fold in half.

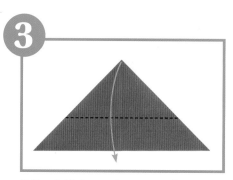

Valley fold the top layer past the bottom edge.

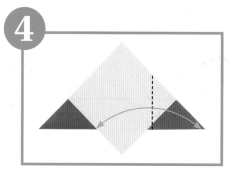

Valley fold to the left edge and unfold.

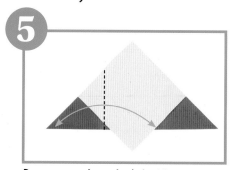

Repeat step 4 on the left side.

6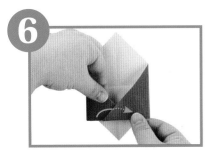

Tuck the left triangle inside the pocket of the right triangle.

7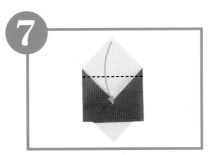

Valley fold slightly past the envelope's opening.

8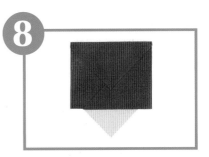

Finished envelope.

BOOKMARK

Traditional Model

Mark your spot in style with this easy-to-make bookmark. You'll never have to worry about losing your place again. These homemade bookmarks also make great gifts for your favorite reader.

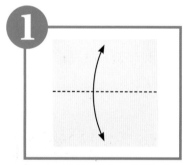

Start with the colored side down.
Valley fold in half and unfold.

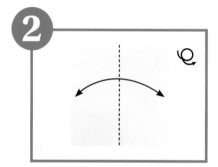

Valley fold in half and unfold.
Rotate the paper.

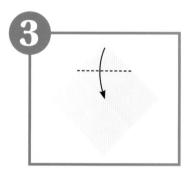

Valley fold to the center crease.

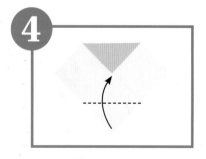

Valley fold to the center crease.

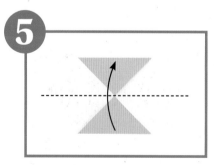

Valley fold in half.

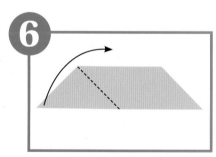

Valley fold along the center crease.

7

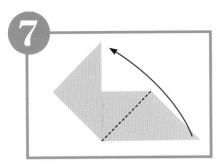

Repeat step 6 on the right side.

8

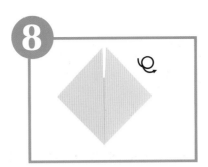

Turn the paper over.

9

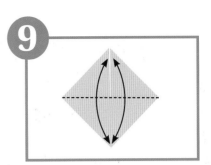

Valley fold both triangle points down and unfold.

10

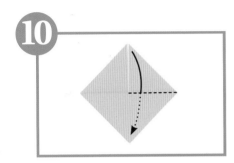

Tuck the top right point into the front pocket.

11

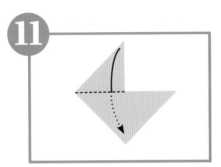

Repeat step 10 on the left side.

12

Finished bookmark.

GLIDING AIRPLANE

Traditional Model

You've probably made a paper airplane before. But did you know you were also making origami? Fold a few of these and challenge your friends to a paper airplane contest. The plane that flies the farthest wins.

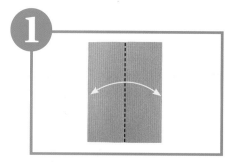

Start with a rectangular sheet of paper. Valley fold in half and unfold.

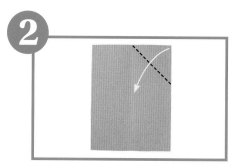

Valley fold to the center crease.

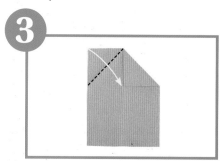

Repeat step 2 on the left side.

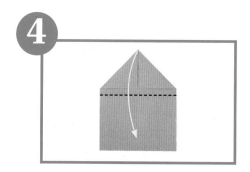

Valley fold 1 inch (2.54 centimeters) from the bottom of the paper.

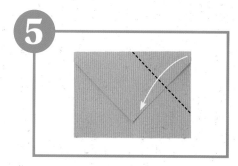

Valley fold to the center crease.

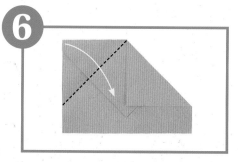

Repeat step 5 on the left side.

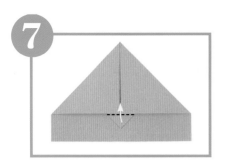

7

Valley fold the mini triangle.

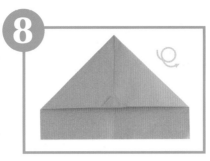

8

Turn the paper over and rotate.

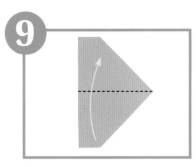

9

Valley fold in half.

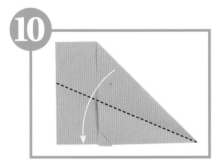

10

Valley fold the top layer along the bottom edge.

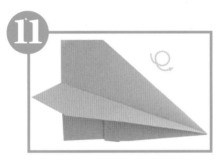

11

Turn the paper over.

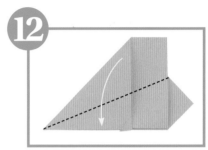

12

Valley fold along the bottom edge.

13

Finished airplane.

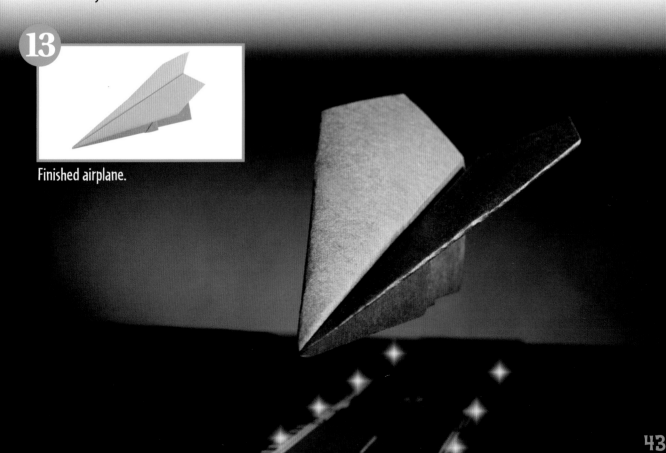

SOMERSAULT SQUARE

Based on a model by Seiro Takekawa

While this model may not look like an acrobat, it sure acts like one. Give it a tap and watch it somersault across a table.

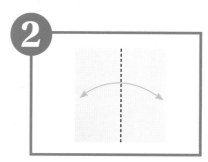

1 Start with the colored side down. Valley fold in half and unfold.

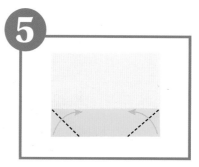

2 Valley fold in half and unfold.

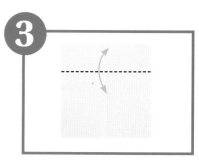

3 Valley fold to the crease made in step 1 and unfold.

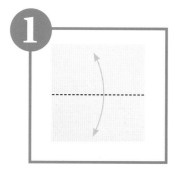

4 Valley fold to the crease made in step 1.

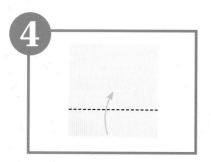

5 Valley fold to the crease made in step 1.

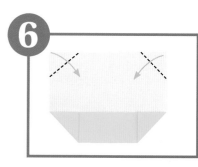

6 Valley fold to the crease made in step 3.

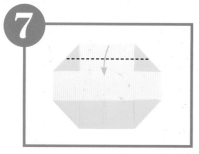

7 Valley fold to the crease made in step 3.

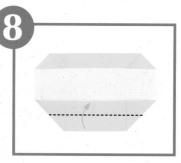

8 Valley fold to the center crease.

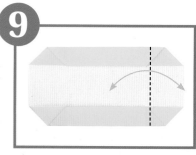

9 Valley fold to the center crease. Unfold halfway.

10

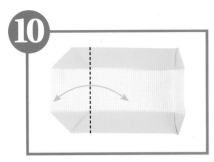

Repeat step 9 on the left side.

11

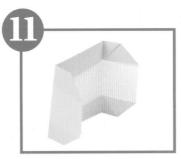

Finished somersault square.
Make sure the thicker side is
on top before using.

Somersault Show
Line up a few somersault squares in a row. Tap the first one over. Watch it knock down the other squares like dominoes.

COASTER

Traditional Model

The next time you have friends over, offer them something to drink. Come back with a tray of drinks and colorful coasters. Two sheets of double-sided paper work best for this project.

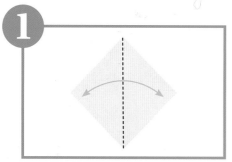

1 Start with the colored side down. Valley fold in half and unfold.

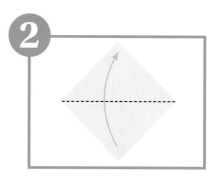

2 Valley fold in half.

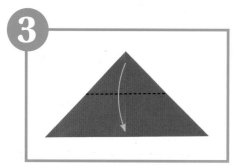

3 Valley fold the top layer to the bottom edge.

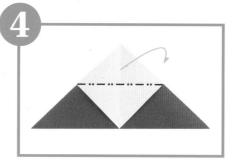

4 Mountain fold the top corner to the bottom edge.

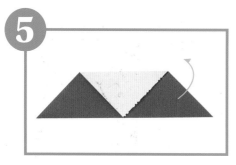

5 Mountain fold to the center crease.

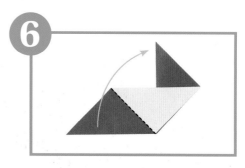

6 Valley fold to the center crease.

7

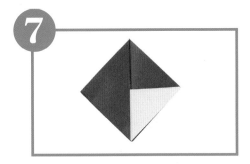

Repeat steps 1 through 6 with another sheet of paper.

8

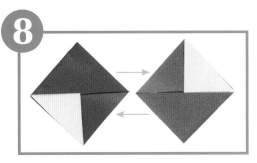

Place the models side-by-side, with the loose triangles facing each other. Slide the models together.

9

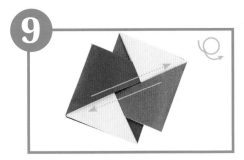

Turn the model over. Tuck the top triangles into the pockets.

10

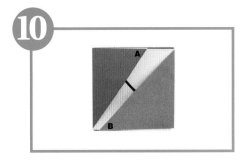

Tuck points A and B into the pockets.

11

Push the two pieces together to make a snug fit.

12

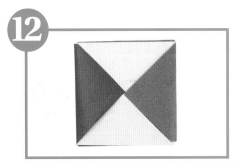

Finished coaster.

47

PINE TREE

Traditional Model

Get lost in a forest of origami trees. Make several trees in different shades of green paper. Change the trunk lengths to create trees that are different shapes and sizes.

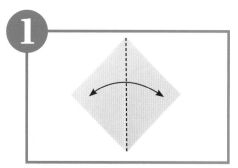

1

Start with the colored side down.
Valley fold in half and unfold.

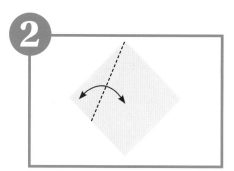

2

Valley fold to the center crease and unfold.

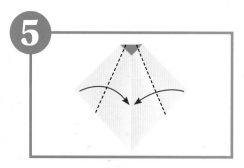

3

Repeat step 2 on the right side.

4

Valley fold the top corner down slightly.

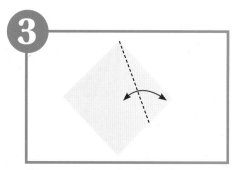

5

Valley fold on the existing creases.

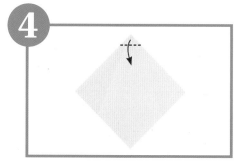

6

Valley fold to the center crease.

7

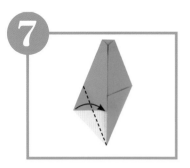

Repeat step 6 on the left side.

8

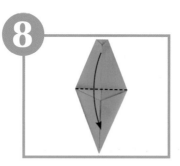

Valley fold.

9

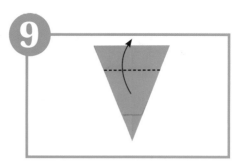

Valley fold the top layer up past the top edge to create the trunk. Tuck the trunk under the flaps beneath it.

10

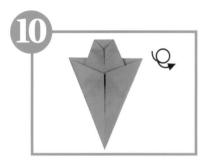

Turn the paper over and rotate.

11

Finished pine tree.

Origami Ornaments
These mini pine trees make great holiday decorations. Punch a hole in the tops and use string to hang them as ornaments.

CICADA

Traditional Model

The cicada origami model has been folded for centuries. In many Asian cultures, these insects are symbols of good fortune. Make your own origami cicada for a good luck charm.

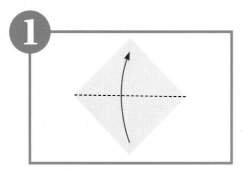

1

Start with the colored side down.
Valley fold the paper in half.

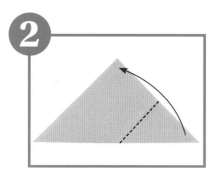

2

Valley fold to the point.

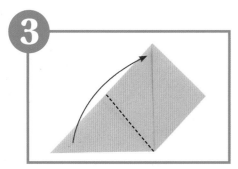

3

Repeat step 2 on the left side.

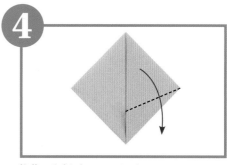

4

Valley fold the top tip down.

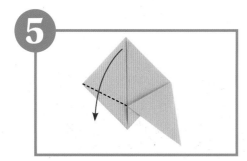

5

Repeat step 4 on the left side.

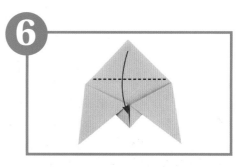

6

Valley fold the top layer. Leave part of the tail showing.

7

Valley fold. Leave part of the white edge showing.

8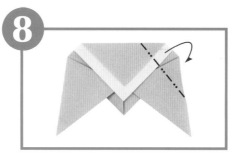

Mountain fold.

9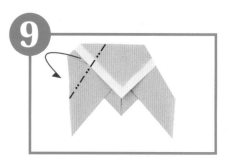

Repeat step 8 on the left side.

10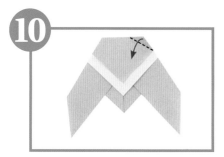

Valley fold to create an eye.

11

Repeat step 10 on the left side.

12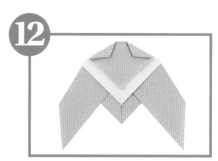

Finished cicada.

51

HOPPING FROG

Traditional Model

Did you know you can play origami leapfrog? To make this model, you will need a rectangular sheet of paper. This model works best if made from stiff paper, such as a recipe card or construction paper.

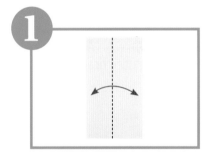

1 Start with the white side up. Valley fold in half and unfold.

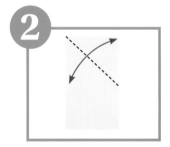

2 Valley fold to meet the left edge and unfold.

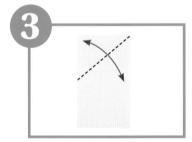

3 Valley fold to meet the right edge and unfold.

4 Turn the paper over.

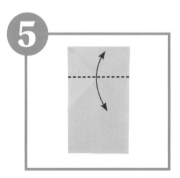

5 Valley fold to meet the edge of the crease and unfold.

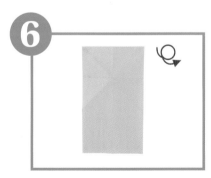

6 Turn the paper over.

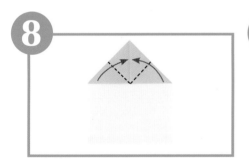

7

Squash fold using the creases formed in steps 2 through 5.

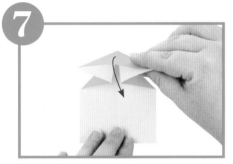

8

Valley fold to the center crease.

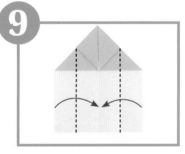

9

Valley fold to the center crease.

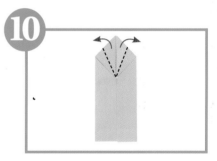

10

Valley fold the top triangles outward.

11

Valley fold to the top point.

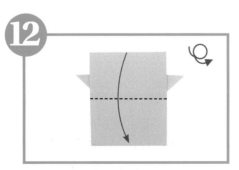

12

Valley fold to the bottom edge. Then turn the model over.

13

Finished frog.

PINWHEEL

Traditional Model

Making a pinwheel is fun and easy. It's no wonder they've been popular toys for more than 100 years. A pinwheel spins by blowing on it. Out of breath? Let the wind do the work for you.

1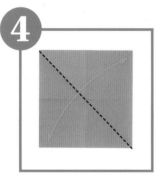

Start with the colored side down. Valley fold in half and unfold.

2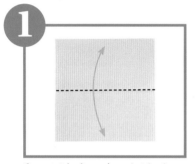

Valley fold in half and unfold.

3

Turn the paper over.

4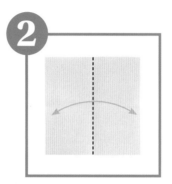

Valley fold in half and unfold.

5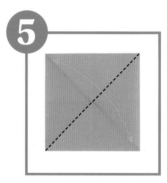

Valley fold in half and unfold.

6

Turn the paper over.

7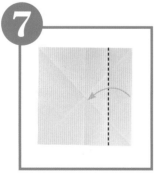

Valley fold to the center crease.

8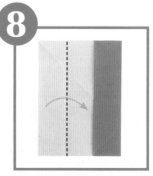

Repeat step 7 on the left side.

9

Valley fold corners to the center crease and unfold.

10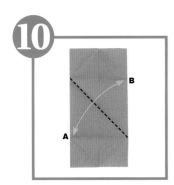

Valley fold point A to point B and unfold.

11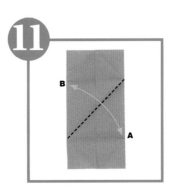

Valley fold point A to point B and unfold.

12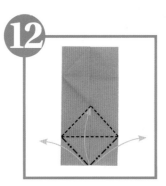

Valley fold bottom edge to the center. Allow the side triangles to squash fold out to the sides.

13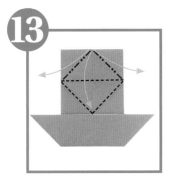

Repeat step 12 on the top.

14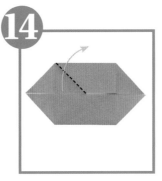

Valley fold to the center crease.

15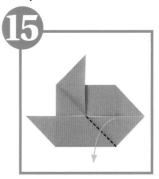

Valley fold to the center crease.

16

Finished pinwheel.

How to Use

To create the pinwheels shown below, use a pushpin to stick the pinwheel onto a straw. Blow on the pinwheel and watch it spin.

FLAPPING CRANE

Traditional Model

The traditional paper crane is perhaps the most popular origami model. This version of the paper crane flaps its wings. Just pull on the tail to see it fly.

1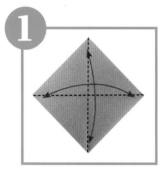
Start with the colored side up. Valley fold in half both ways and unfold.

2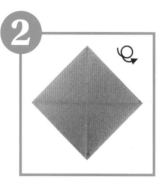
Turn the paper over.

3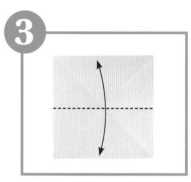
Valley fold in half and unfold.

4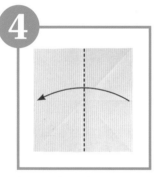
Valley fold in half.

5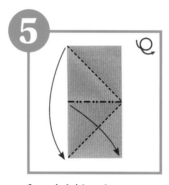
Squash fold and rotate.

6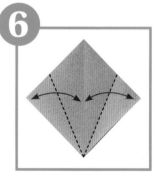
Valley fold the top layer to the center crease and unfold.

7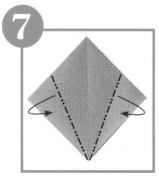
Reverse fold on the creases formed in step 6.

8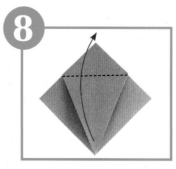
Valley fold the point up.

9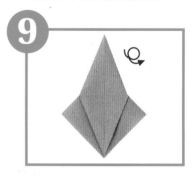
Turn the paper over.

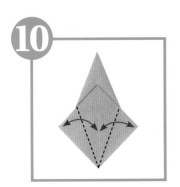

10 Repeat steps 6 through 8.

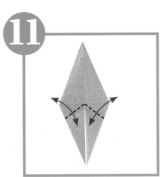

11 Valley fold and unfold.

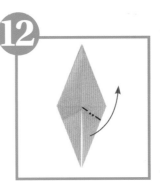

12 Reverse fold along the crease formed in step 11.

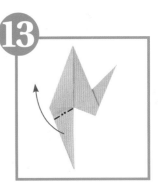

13 Repeat step 12 on the left side.

14 Reverse fold to create the crane's head.

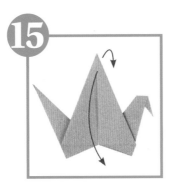

15 Gently bend down the wings.

16 Finished crane.

Fly, Fly Birdie

Watch this bird try to fly away. Hold on to the point just below the bird's head. Gently tug on the tail to make the wings flap.

FUN FACTS

The world's smallest origami model was of the pajarita bird. In 1993, Lluis Valldeneu i Bigas, a Spanish watchmaker, folded the bird out of paper measuring just over one hundredth of an inch (0.3 millimeters) on each side. He used two pairs of tweezers and a magnifying glass to accomplish this tiny task. The finished bird was the size of the period at the end of this sentence.

World Origami Days is celebrated October 24 through November 11. American origami pioneer Lillian Oppenheimer's birthday is on October 24. November 11 is Japan's traditional Origami Day. During this time, people around the world fold origami models and teach others their techniques.

On October 23, 2004, Akie Morita broke a world record by folding 100 paper cranes in just 98 minutes.

In 1955, 11-year-old Sadako Sasaki developed a type of cancer called leukemia. Sadako knew of a legend that said anyone who folded 1,000 paper cranes would be granted a wish. She went to work folding cranes so she could wish to get well. But she was too ill and died after making only 645 cranes. Her classmates finished the remaining 355 cranes. A statue of Sadako holding a paper crane stands in Hiroshima's Peace Park.

WHAT'S NEXT...

You've practiced your folding skills on all of the not-quite-so-easy projects in this book. Are you ready to try some more difficult projects? Then check out the sort-of-difficult projects. They are sure to put your skills to the test.

In the sort-of-difficult projects, you'll learn how to make tulips, penguins, seals, and more. New folds are introduced, and the projects have more steps. The models are challenging, but your practice will pay off.

Chapter Three

sort-of-difficult
ORIGAMI
projects

SORT-OF-DIFFICULT PROJECTS

Now it's time to step up your folding skills. The seal, penguin, tulip, and other models are challenging. But the finished models will definitely amaze your friends and family.

To get started, all you'll need are square pieces of paper and a little patience. Remember, practice is the key to success. If your model doesn't turn out the way it should, don't worry. Crumple it up and tell your friends you've made a basketball. Then score two points in the recycle bin and try the model again. The more times you practice a model, the better it will look.

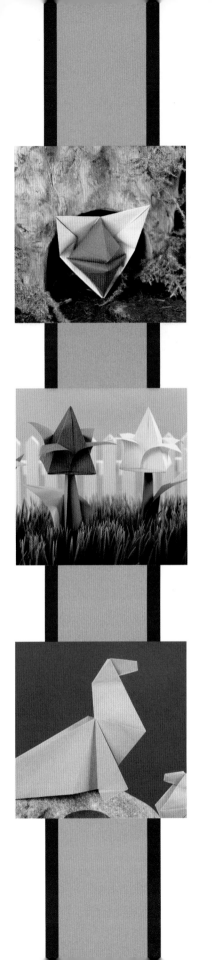

Two folds to review

Outside reverse folds are two valley folds done at once. They are made by folding the model outside itself along existing creases.

Rabbit ear folds are formed by bringing two edges of a point together using existing creases. The new point is folded to one side.

FOX MASK

Traditional Model

Many origami models are flat and solid colored. The fox mask uses the white side of a colored piece of paper to highlight the ears. As an added bonus, the fox mask is an action model.

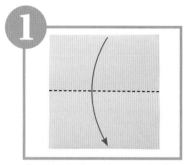

Start with the colored side down.
Valley fold in half.

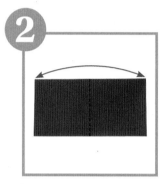

Valley fold in half and unfold.

Valley fold both edges to the center.

Valley fold the top flap to
the left edge and unfold.

Squash fold on the crease
made in step 4.

Repeat steps 4 and 5
on the right side.

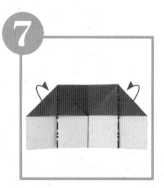

Mountain fold the flaps to
the back of the model.

Rotate the paper.

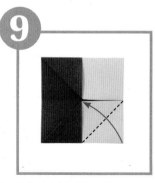

Valley fold the top
layer to the center.

10

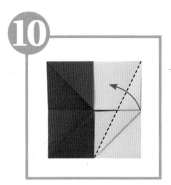

Valley fold. The crease goes from corner to corner. The edge does not meet the center line.

11

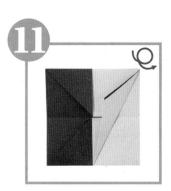

Turn the paper over.

12

Repeat steps 9 and 10 on this side.

13

Valley fold the top flap to the right. Repeat behind.

14

Slowly spread the area marked A open while carefully pressing in at B.

15

Finished fox mask. Put your fingers inside the mask to open and close the mouth.

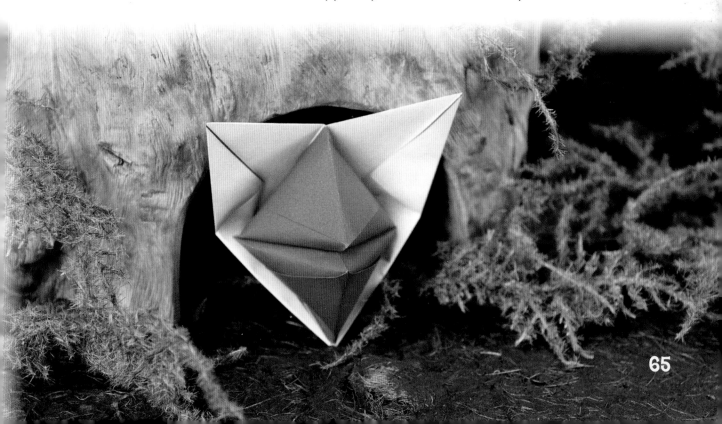

WATERBOMB

Traditional Model

The waterbomb model has been around for hundreds of years. Originally, it was filled with water and tossed like a water balloon. The model can also be used as a ball, an ornament, or dice.

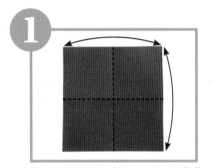

1 Start with the colored side up. Valley fold edge to edge in both directions and unfold.

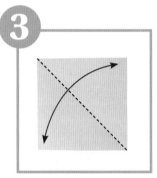

2 Turn the paper over.

3 Valley fold point to point and unfold.

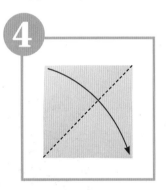

4 Valley fold point to point.

5 Squash fold.

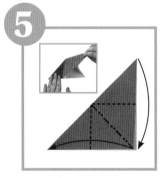

6 Valley fold the top flap to the peak.

7 Mark fold the top flap in half and unfold.

8 Valley fold the corner to the mark made in step 7.

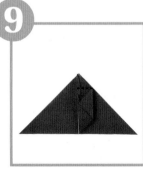

9 Valley fold the top point to the corner made in step 8.

10

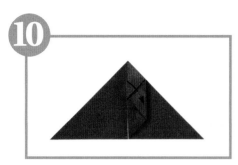

Valley fold the entire triangle into
the pocket made in step 8.

11

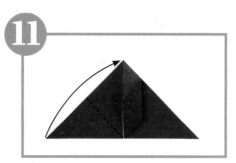

Repeat steps 6 through 10
on the left side.

12

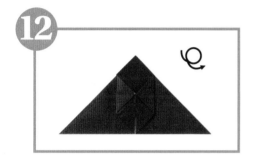

Turn the model over.

13

Repeat steps 6 through 11
on this side.

14

Valley fold to the
center and unfold.

15

Gently blow into the hole
at A to inflate the model.

16

Finished waterbomb.

ORNAMENT

Traditional Model

Modular origami models, like this ornament, are made from several sheets of paper. As a rule, each sheet is folded into the same basic unit. Then the units are assembled together without using glue.

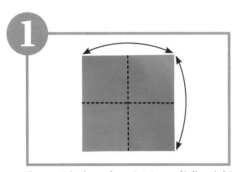

1 Start with the colored side up. Valley fold edge to edge in both directions and unfold.

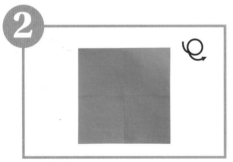

2 Turn the paper over.

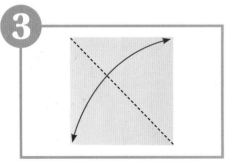

3 Valley fold point to point and unfold.

4

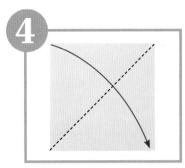

Valley fold point to point.

5

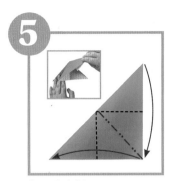

Squash fold.

6

Spread the points apart so it looks like an X from above.

7

Finished waterbomb unit. Repeat steps 1 through 6 to make five more units.

8

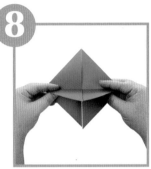

Place two units together so all four edges touch.

9

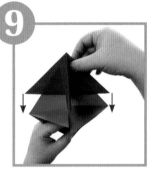

Place one unit over the top two points.

10

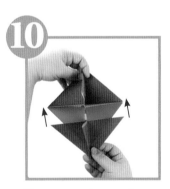

Place one unit over the bottom two points.

11

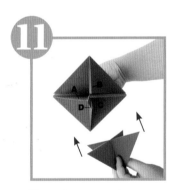

Place the next unit over points A and C.

12

Place point A into the pocket of point B.

13

Place point C into the pocket of point D.

14

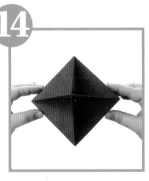

Repeat steps 11 through 13 with the last unit on the points in the back.

15

Finished ornament.

TULIP AND STEM

Traditional Model

Origami artists have invented many ways to fold tulips. This model is fun because it inflates like a balloon. Bring your tulip to life by mounting it on a stem.

Part 1: The Tulip

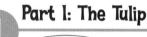

1

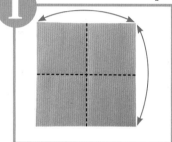

Start with the colored side up. Valley fold edge to edge in both directions and unfold.

2

Turn the paper over.

3

Valley fold point to point and unfold.

4

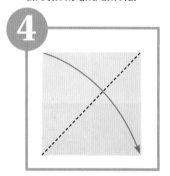

Valley fold point to point.

5

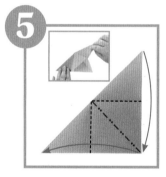

Squash fold.

6

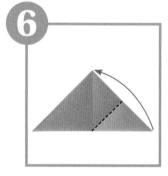

Valley fold the top flap to the peak.

7

Valley fold the top flap to the peak.

8

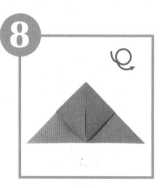

Turn the model over.

9

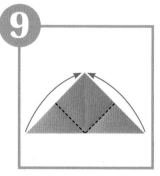

Repeat steps 6 and 7 on this side.

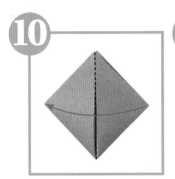

10 Valley fold the top flap from right to left.

11 Turn the model over.

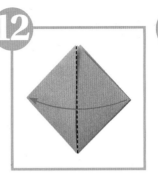

12 Valley fold the top flap from right to left.

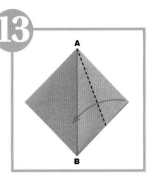

13 Valley fold the corner just past the center line AB.

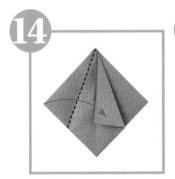

14 Repeat step 13 on the left side. Insert the corner of the top flap into the pocket.

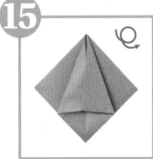

15 Turn the model over.

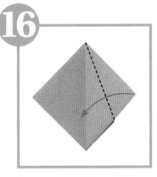

16 Repeat steps 13 and 14 on this side.

17 Valley fold and unfold.

18 Gently blow into the model at A forming a tall pyramid.

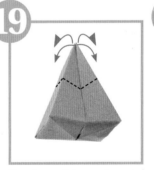

19 Gently peel down the petals like you would peel a banana.

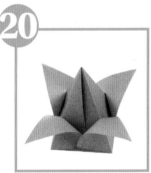

20 Finished tulip.

Part 2: The Stem

1

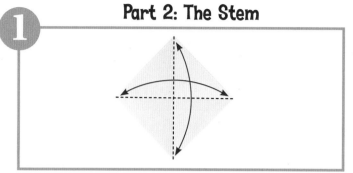

Start with the colored side down. Valley fold point to point in both directions and unfold.

2

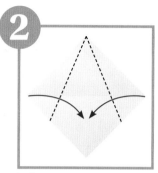

Valley fold both edges to the center.

3

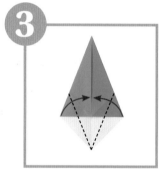

Valley fold both edges to the center.

4

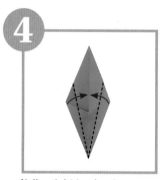

Valley fold both edges to the center.

5

Valley fold in half.

6

Valley fold in half.

7

Gently peel down the leaf like you would peel a banana.

8

Finished stem. Insert the stem into the blow hole of the tulip to display your flower.

MASU BOX AND INSERT

Traditional Model

Here is a simple project for storing your tiny keepsakes. Start with three pieces of paper, all the same size. One will be used for the insert, and the other two for the box and its lid.

① Part I: The Box and Lid

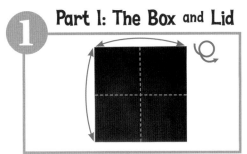

Start with the colored side up. Valley fold edge to edge in both directions and unfold. Then turn the paper over.

②

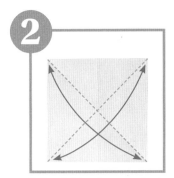

Valley fold point to point in both directions and unfold.

③

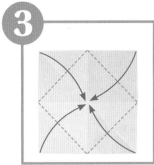

For a box, valley fold the corners to the center. For a lid, valley fold ⅛ of an inch from the center.

④

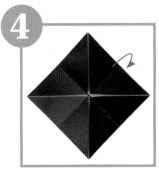

Mountain fold in half.

⑤

Valley fold the top layer in half. Repeat behind.

⑥

Unfold to step 4.

⑦

Repeat steps 4 through 6 on the opposite edges.

⑧

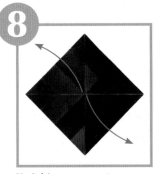

Unfold two opposite corners.

⑨

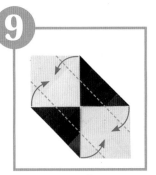

Valley fold to allow two sides of the box to stand up.

73

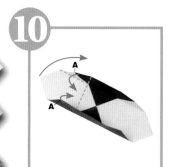

10 Fold up the third side of the box. The corners marked A will fold in against the inside of the box.

11 Valley fold the side in half and push the point into the center of the box.

12 Repeat steps 10 and 11 on the last side of the box.

13 Finished masu box.

Part 2: The Insert

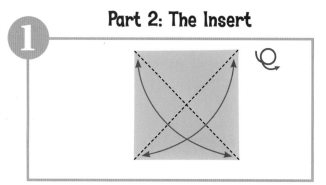

1 Start with the colored side up. Valley fold point to point in both directions and unfold. Then turn the paper over.

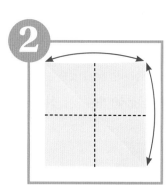

2 Valley fold edge to edge in both directions and unfold.

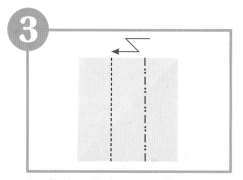

3 Gently pleat the paper into thirds. Adjust the paper until all three panels are equal, then crease sharply.

4 Unfold to step 3.

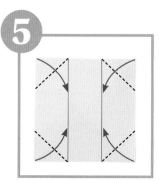

5 Valley fold the corners to the creases made in step 3.

6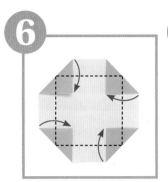

Valley fold the edges even with the corners.

7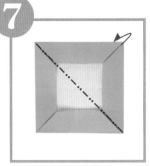

Mountain fold in half.

8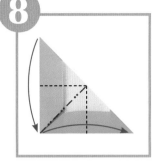

Squash fold on the creases made in steps 1 and 2.

9

Valley fold the peak to the bottom edge.

10

Unfold the flap under the triangle. The model will be three dimensional.

11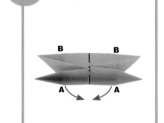

Mountain fold in half. This joins the two As and the two Bs together.

12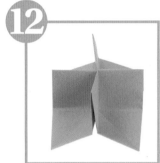

Reshape and reinforce all of the creases so the model will sit in the box.

13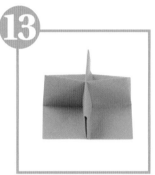

Finished insert. Place into the masu box.

FANCY GOLDFISH

Model designed by Chris Alexander

Some fancy goldfish can cost as much as $15,000. This model of a fancy goldfish will cost you only one square of paper. The finished model will be well worth the expense.

1
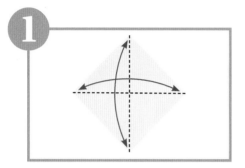
Start with the colored side down. Valley fold point to point in both directions and unfold.

2
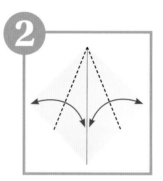
Valley fold the edges to the center and unfold.

3
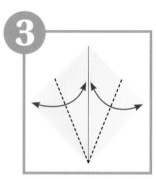
Valley fold the edges to the center and unfold.

4
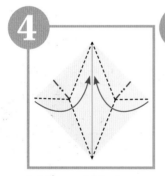
Rabbit ear fold using the creases made in steps 2 and 3.

5

Mountain fold the bottom point. The point should be even with the tips of the flaps.

6
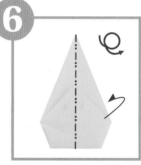
Mountain fold in half. Then rotate the model.

7

Valley fold and unfold. This crease starts about ⅓ of the way up the left edge.

8
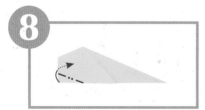
Reverse fold on the crease made in step 7.

9
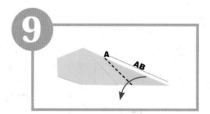
Valley fold so edge AB meets the tip of the flap.

10
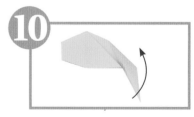
Unfold to step 9.

11

Valley fold the edge to the crease line and unfold. Repeat behind.

12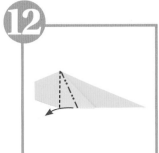

Squash fold to form the fin. Repeat behind.

13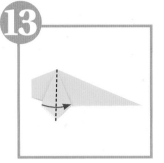

Valley fold the fin in half. Repeat behind.

14

Valley fold the top layer to the edge. Repeat behind.

15

Valley fold the flap back to the left. Repeat behind.

16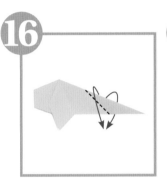

Outside reverse fold on the crease made in step 9.

17

Pull out the hidden paper inside the tail and place it on top of the tail. Repeat behind.

18

Valley fold the flap made in step 17 to the left. Repeat behind.

19

Finished fancy goldfish.

SEAL

Traditional Model

Seals can learn to perform all sorts of tricks. Likewise, this origami seal has a few tricks of its own to teach you. To complete the model, you'll need to perform several reverse folds.

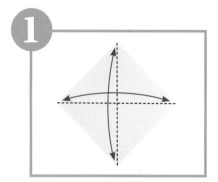

1 Start with the colored side down. Valley fold point to point in both directions and unfold.

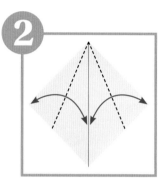

2 Valley fold both edges to the center and unfold.

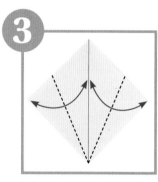

3 Valley fold both edges to the center and unfold.

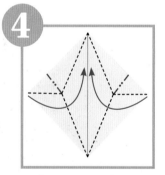

4 Rabbit ear fold using the creases made in steps 2 and 3.

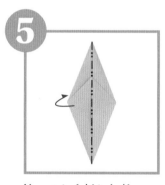

5 Mountain fold in half.

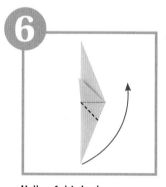

6 Valley fold the lower point to the right.

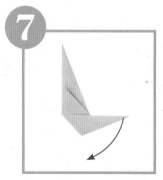

7 Unfold.

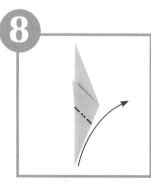

8 Reverse fold on the crease made in step 6.

9 Rotate the model.

10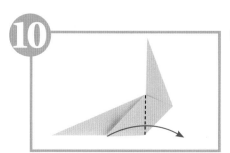

Valley fold the flap to the right. Repeat behind.

11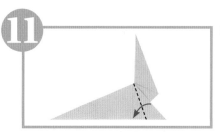

Valley fold the edge to the crease made in step 10. Repeat behind.

12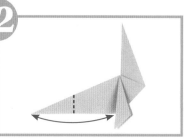

Mark fold the tip to the edge of the flipper and unfold.

13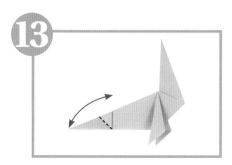

Mark fold the edge to the mark made in step 12 and unfold.

14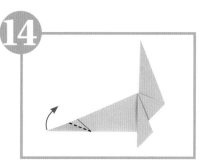

Valley fold the edge to the mark made in step 13.

15

Unfold.

16

Reverse fold using the crease made in step 14.

17

Mark fold the point to about halfway between A and B.

18

Unfold to step 17.

19

Valley fold to the mark made in step 17 and unfold.

20

Reverse fold using the crease made in step 19.

21

Valley fold even with the chest and unfold.

22

Reverse fold using the crease made in step 21.

23

Valley fold the flippers outward so the model stands.

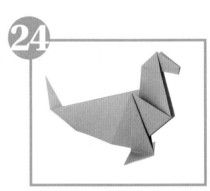

24

Finished seal.

PENGUIN

Traditional Model

Penguins are well adapted to life in the Antarctic. They can't fly, but their flipper-like wings make them strong swimmers. Folding the wings on this model will strengthen your origami skills. To form them, you'll practice a challenging rabbit ear fold.

1

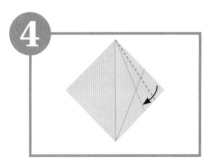

Start with the colored side down. Valley fold point to point and unfold.

2

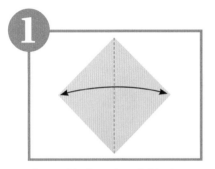

Valley fold to the center and unfold.

3

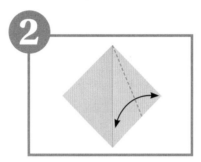

Valley fold to the center and unfold.

4

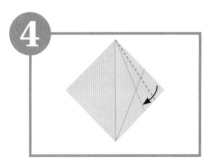

Valley fold to the crease made in step 2.

5

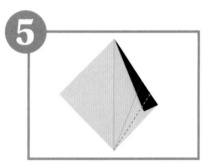

Valley fold to the crease made in step 3.

6

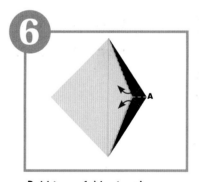

Rabbit ear fold using the creases made in steps 2 and 3. Carefully pinch the paper together at point A and lay it flat.

7

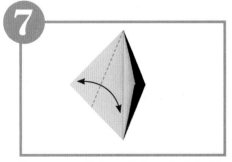

Repeat steps 2 through 6 on the left side.

8

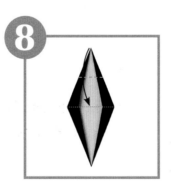

Valley fold the point to the center of the model.

9

Mark fold the point even with the tips of the wings and unfold.

10

Mountain fold the model in half.

11

Rotate the figure so edge AB is straight up and down.

12

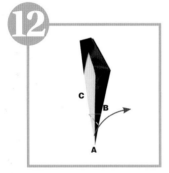

Valley fold. Edge AB forms a right angle with edge AC. The crease starts at the mark made in step 9.

13

Valley fold even with edge B.

14

Unfold to step 12.

15

Reverse fold on the crease made in step 12.

16

Reverse fold on the crease made in step 13.

17

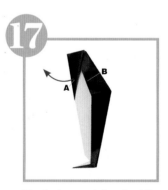

Pinch the model at B while pivoting A out to the left.

18 Valley fold the tip of the beak to the back of the head and unfold.

19 Valley fold the tip of the beak to the white corner and unfold.

20 Reverse fold on the crease made in step 18. Then reverse fold on the crease made in step 19.

21 Finished penguin.

FUN FACTS

In 2001, the largest paper crane was folded in the Odate Jukai Dome in Maebashi, Japan. It had a wingspan of 256 feet (78 meters).

The Red Sea Urchin, designed by Hans Birkeland, uses the most folds for a single model. The paper must be folded 913 times to create the model.

In 1967, the British Origami Society in London became the first organized origami society. OrigamiUSA formed in the United States in 1980.

The largest number of units used in a modular origami model is 2,200 units. These units form a wall mosaic showing the swan logo of the Origami Society Netherlands.

OrigamiUSA holds a convention each summer in New York City. The convention attracts origami masters and fans from all over the world. The convention gives people a chance see amazing origami models and learn more about the art.

Some people fold origami to express other hobbies and interests in their lives. Chris Alexander, the co-author of this book, creates models of the characters and spaceships from the *Star Wars* movies.

WHAT'S NEXT. . .

Now that you've mastered these sort-of-difficult models, it's time to move on to more challenging projects. Next is difficult origami. You'll learn how to make a lop-eared rabbit, a speedboat, a picture frame, and many other models.

Visit your local library and check out books by other artists. You will be amazed by what you can create with a simple piece of paper and a little imagination. Who knows? With enough practice you may become an origami master.

Chapter Four

difficult
ORIGAMI
projects

DIFFICULT PROJECTS

Welcome to the big leagues! If you've completed the previous projects in this book, you're ready for a new challenge. Now you will fine-tune the folding skills you've learned so far. These difficult models have more steps, which require greater skill to complete.

So what kind of models will you find in the coming pages? You'll make a cat with a curved tail, a frog that inflates, and several other great projects. And as you master these models, experiment with them. Try making them from different types of paper. See if you can change the crested bird into a dragon. Don't be afraid to experiment with the steps. Origami is an art form. Let your inner artist shine.

Meet Chris Alexander

Chris Alexander made the sort-of-difficult and difficult projects in this book. He was born and raised in New York City. At the age of 5, he had his first experience with origami. During a visit to the public library, he came across a book with simple folding instructions. After successfully completing a paper cup, he was instantly hooked on the art. He has created approximately 100 original origami models.

SPEEDBOAT

Traditional Model

This speedboat is a variation of an origami canoe. If you set the boat in water and blow on it, the boat will zip along nicely.

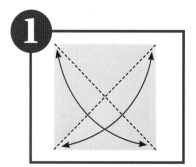

Start with the colored side down. Valley fold point to point in both directions and unfold.

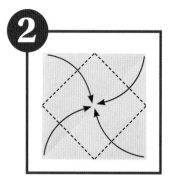

Valley fold the corners to the center.

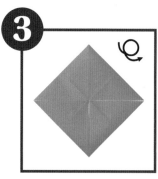

Turn the model over.

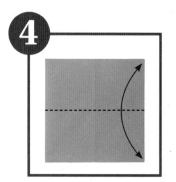

Valley fold in half and unfold.

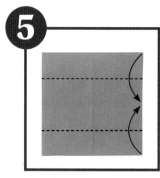

Valley fold the edges to the center.

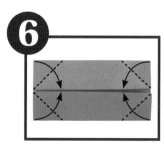

Valley fold the corners to the center.

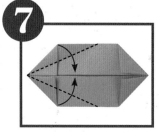

Valley fold to the center.

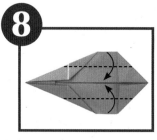

Valley fold to the center.

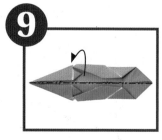

Mountain fold in half.

10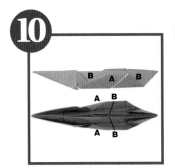

Spread the model open by holding flaps A and B together and pulling them away from the center.

11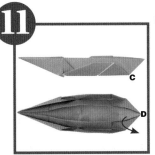

Now push corner C inside out. Pinch the paper at D to keep it from tearing.

12

Keep pinching D while pushing the second corner inside out. Allow the hidden tail fin to pop outward.

13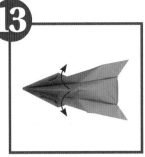

Continue rolling the sides from the back to the front until the sides are fully formed.

14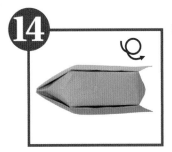

Shape and reinforce all of the creases, then turn the boat right side up.

15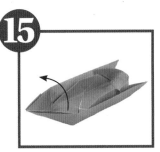

Lift up the front flap.

16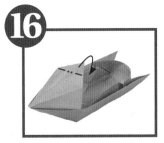

Mountain fold the top third of the flap inside the model.

17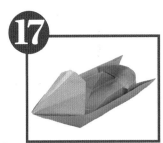

Finished speedboat.

LILY

Traditional Model

Lilies come in a variety of colors ranging from pink to black. This origami lily looks very pretty when folded with paper that has colored corners.

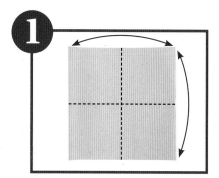

1 Start with the colored side up. Valley fold edge to edge in both directions and unfold.

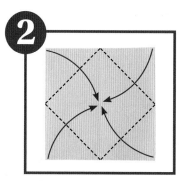

2 Valley fold the corners to the center.

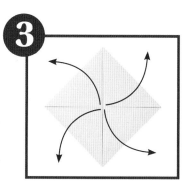

3 Unfold the corners.

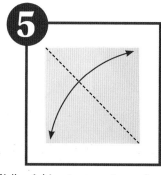

4 Turn the paper over.

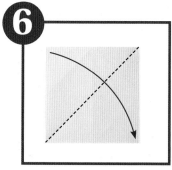

5 Valley fold point to point and unfold.

6 Valley fold point to point.

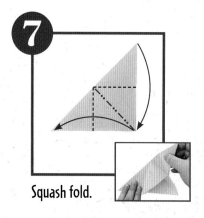

7 Squash fold.

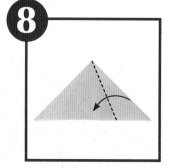

8 Valley fold the top flap to the center crease.

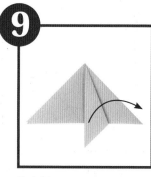

9 Unfold to step 8.

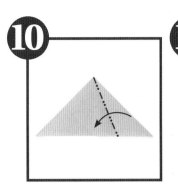 **10**

Squash fold the top flap.

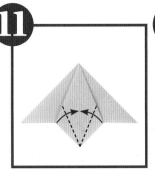 **11**

Valley fold both edges to the center.

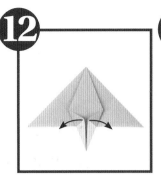 **12**

Unfold to step 11.

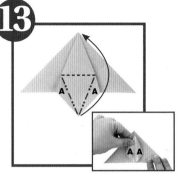 **13**

Lift the point to the peak, allowing A to fold inward.

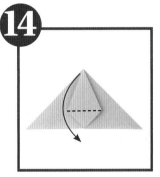 **14**

Valley fold the point down.

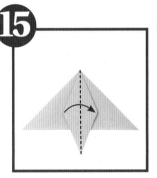 **15**

Valley fold the left flap to the right.

 **16**

Repeat steps 8 through 15 on the left side.

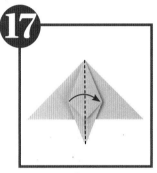 **17**

Valley fold the left side to the right.

 **18**

Turn the model over.

 **19**

Repeat steps 8 through 17 on this side.

93

20

Rotate the model so the four points are on top.

21

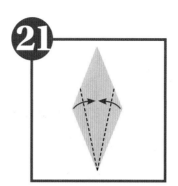

Valley fold the top flaps to the center.

22

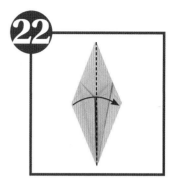

Valley fold the top two flaps to the right.

23

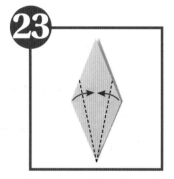

Repeat step 21 on this side.

24

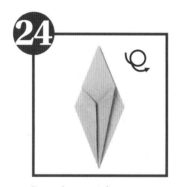

Turn the model over.

25

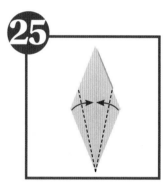

Repeat steps 21 through 23 on this side.

26

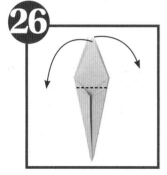

Valley fold the top petal halfway down. Repeat on the back petal.

27

Valley fold the remaining two petals halfway down.

28

Finished lily.

CATNIP THE CAT

Model designed by Chris Alexander

The ancient Egyptians believed cats were living gods. Judging by their attitudes, most cats still feel this way today. An extremely proud cat named Catnip inspired this model.

①

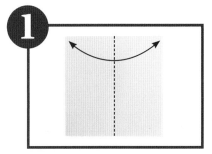

Start with the colored side down. Valley fold in half and unfold.

②

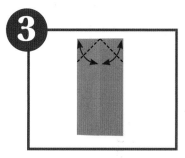

Valley fold the edges to the center.

③

Valley fold the corners to the center and unfold.

④

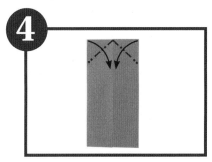

Reverse fold on the creases formed in step 3.

⑤

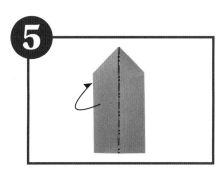

Mountain fold the left side behind the right side.

⑥

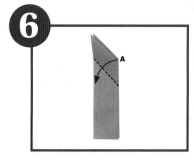

Valley fold corner A to the edge.

⑦

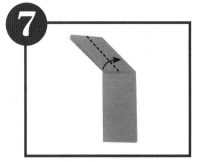

Valley fold in half.

⑧

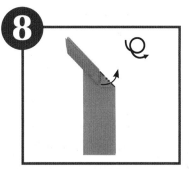

Unfold the crease formed in step 6, then turn the model over.

⑨

Unfold the top layer to the left and squash fold the hidden triangle.

95

10

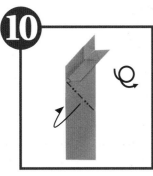

Mountain fold, forming a right angle at the corner. Turn the model over.

11

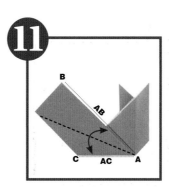

Valley fold edge AB even with edge AC and unfold.

12

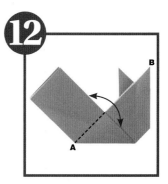

Valley fold even with edge AB and unfold.

13

Rabbit ear fold on the creases made in steps 11 and 12.

14

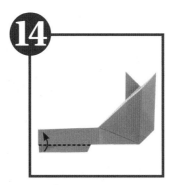

Valley fold the exposed section of the tail.

15

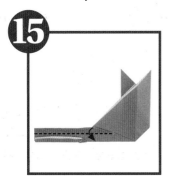

Valley fold the tail in half.

16

Valley fold the ear down even with the top of the head.

17

Valley fold about ¾ of the way back up.

Unfold to step 16.

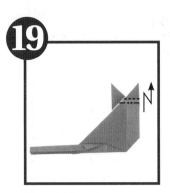

Pleat fold on the creases formed in steps 16 and 17.

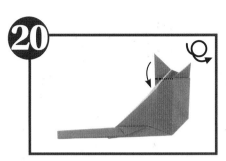

Repeat steps 16 through 19 on the other ear, then turn the model over.

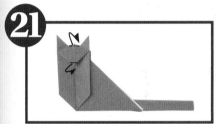

Mountain fold the tip of the nose and the top of the head.

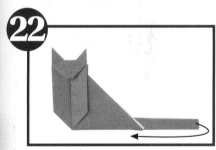

Curl the tail so the model will stand.

Finished cat.

PICTURE FRAME

Model designed by Chris Alexander

This three-dimensional frame will highlight almost any size picture. Start with a square sheet of paper at least 50 percent larger than the long side of the picture.

1

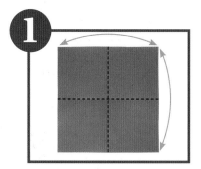

Start with the colored side up. Mark fold from edge to edge in both directions and unfold.

2

Using the creases for alignment, center the picture on the paper.

3

Valley fold even with the edge of the picture and unfold.

4

Valley fold and unfold the other three sides.

5

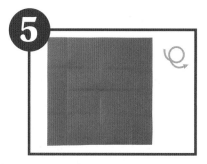

Remove the picture and turn the paper over.

6

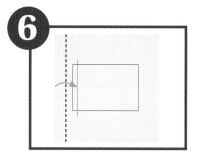

Valley fold the paper about ¼ of an inch over the crease.

7

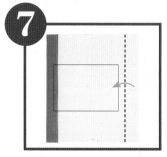

Valley fold the paper about ¼ of an inch over the crease.

8

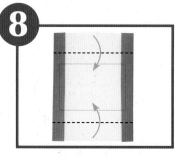

Valley fold the paper about ¼ of an inch over the crease.

9

Turn the paper over.

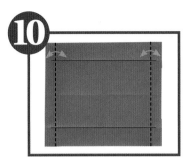

10

Valley fold on the creases formed in steps 3 and 4 and unfold.

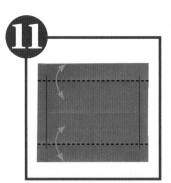

11

Valley fold on the creases formed in step 4 and unfold.

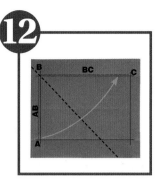

12

Valley fold crease AB even with crease BC.

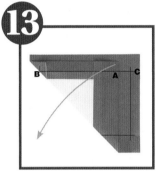

13

Unfold.

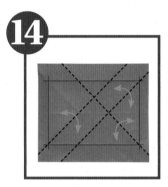

14

Repeat steps 12 and 13 on the other three corners.

15

Valley fold even with the ends of the creases formed in steps 12 and 14 and unfold.

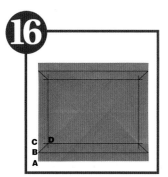

16

If the distance between A and B is smaller than between C and D, skip to step 18.

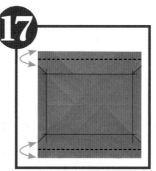

17

Valley fold only if AB was larger than CD in step 16.

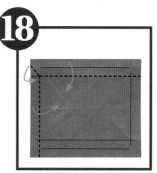

18

Rabbit ear fold to form a boxlike corner.

19

Valley fold the extended flap even with the back side of the box.

20

Repeat steps 16 through 19 on the other three corners.

21

Unfold the model completely. Place the picture inside and refold everything up to this step.

22

Valley fold on the crease formed in step 15.

23

Repeat step 22 on this side.

24

Stand up the frame.

25

Finished picture frame.

LOP-EARED RABBIT

Model designed by Chris Alexander

Lop-eared rabbits have long, floppy ears that hang down and touch the ground. This unique feature gives this model a comic personality.

1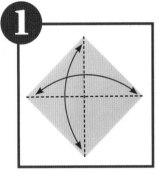

Start with the colored side up. Valley fold point to point in both directions and unfold.

2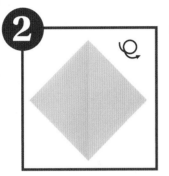

Turn the paper over.

3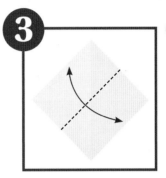

Valley fold edge to edge and unfold.

4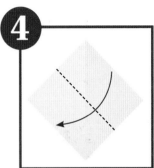

Valley fold edge to edge.

5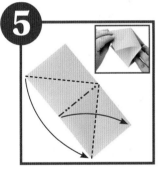

Squash fold.

6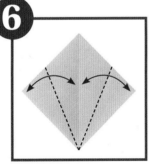

Valley fold the top flaps to the center and unfold. Repeat behind.

7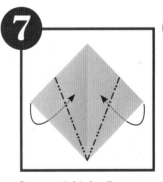

Reverse fold the flaps. Repeat behind.

8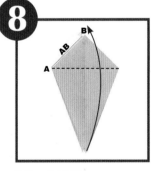

Valley fold. Note edge AB for step 9.

9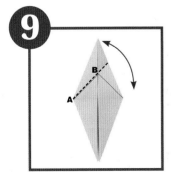

Valley fold the left side on the hidden edge and unfold. Repeat on right side.

10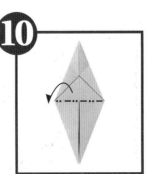

Mountain fold the triangle in the back all the way down.

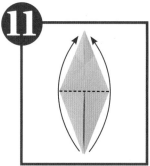

11 Valley fold the two points up.

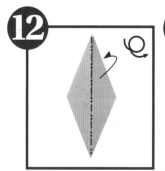

12 Mountain fold and rotate the model.

13 Valley fold the top flap even with the crease formed in step 9. Repeat behind.

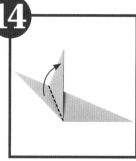

14 Valley fold even with the crease formed in step 13.

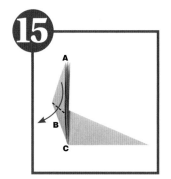

15 Valley fold so A, B, and C form a right angle.

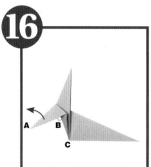

16 Unfold to step 14.

17 Squash fold on the creases formed in steps 14 and 15.

18 Valley fold the point so it almost reaches the corner.

19 Unfold the point.

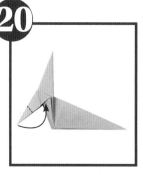

20 Reverse fold on the crease formed in step 18.

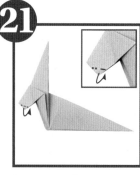

21 Mountain fold into the head. Repeat behind.

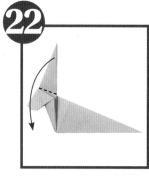

22 Valley fold the ear. Repeat behind.

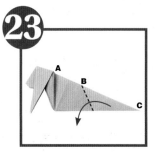

23 Valley fold so A, B, and C form a right angle.

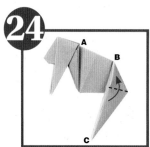

24 Valley fold even with edge CB.

25 Valley fold even with the edge formed in step 23.

26 Valley fold even with the edge formed in step 24.

27

Unfold to step 23.

28

Reverse fold on the creases formed in steps 23 and 24.

29

Squash fold on the creases formed in steps 25 and 26.

30

Valley fold in half and unfold.

31

Reverse fold on the crease formed in step 30.

32

Tuck flap A inside the back of the body. Repeat behind.

33

Finished lop-eared rabbit.

CRESTED BIRD

Model designed by Chris Alexander

The unique feature of this bird is a feather crest on the top of its head. This basic bird model represents crested birds such as the long-crested eagle or the crested goshawk.

1
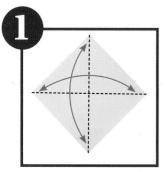
Start with the colored side up. Valley fold point to point in both directions and unfold.

2

Turn the paper over.

3
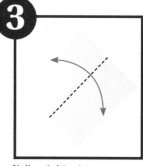
Valley fold edge to edge and unfold.

4
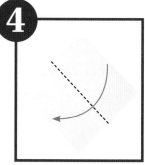
Valley fold edge to edge.

5
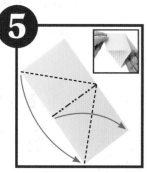
Squash fold.

6
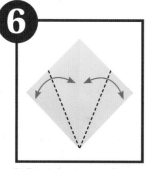
Valley fold the top flaps to the center and unfold. Repeat behind.

7
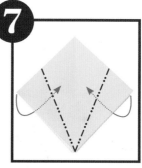
Reverse fold the flaps. Repeat behind.

8
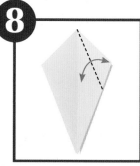
Valley fold the top flap to the center and unfold.

9
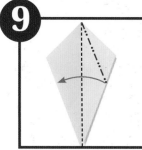
Squash fold on the crease formed in step 8.

10
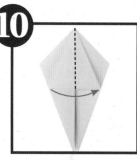
Valley fold the top flap to the right side.

11
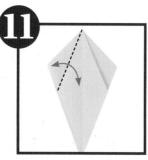
Repeat steps 8 through 10 on the left side.

12

Turn the model over.

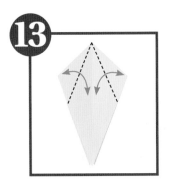

Repeat steps 8 through 11 on this side.

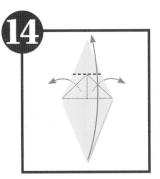

Valley fold the top flap up as far as it will go. Allow the hidden triangles to unfold.

Valley fold the top flaps.

Unfold the flaps.

Reverse fold the top flaps on the creases formed in step 15.

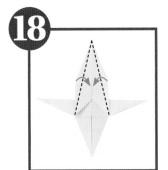

Valley fold. The creases go from point to corner and do not meet in the center.

Unfold the top flaps.

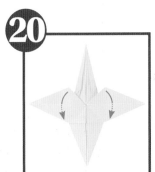

Insert the top flaps into the pockets of the bottom flaps.

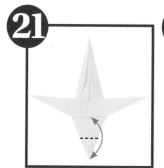

21

Valley fold the point to the edge of the wings and unfold.

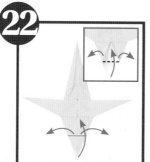

22

Spread the edges apart and valley fold the tip inside the opening.

23

Valley fold the edges outward.

24

Valley fold the point down. The crease starts where the edges meet.

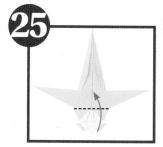

25

Valley fold even with the edge of the wings.

26

Valley fold the head down. Start the crease just above the crease formed in step 25.

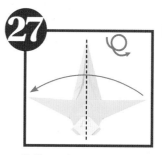

27

Valley fold in half and rotate the model.

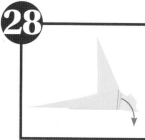

28

Gently pivot the head down.

29

Outside reverse fold to form the legs. There are no guide marks for this step.

30

Outside reverse fold to form the feet. There are no guide marks for this step.

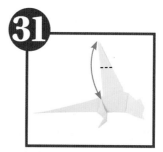

31

Valley fold the tip of the wing to the top of the leg and unfold. Repeat behind.

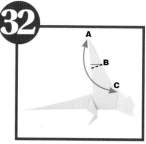

32

Valley fold so edge AB lays on edge BC and unfold. Repeat behind.

33

Pleat fold on the creases formed in steps 31 and 32. Repeat behind.

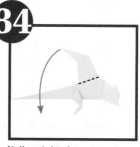

34

Valley fold the wing down. Repeat behind.

35

Finished crested bird.

CLASSIC FROG

Traditional Model

Frogs have inspired many origami models. This version is fun because you inflate the frog when you're done folding. Just try not to laugh when you blow air into its rear end.

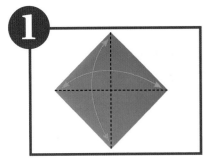

1 Start with the colored side up. Valley fold point to point in both directions and unfold.

2 Turn the paper over.

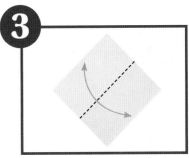

3 Valley fold edge to edge and unfold.

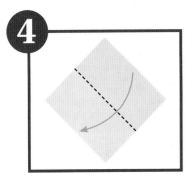

4 Valley fold edge to edge.

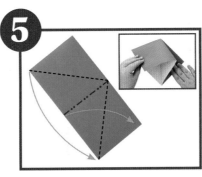

5 Squash fold.

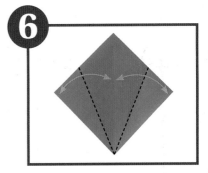

6 Valley fold the top flaps to the center and unfold. Repeat behind.

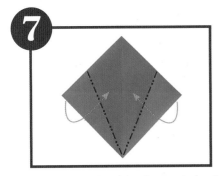

7 Reverse fold the flaps. Repeat behind.

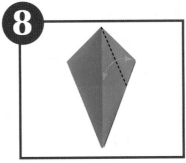

8 Valley fold the top flap to the center and unfold.

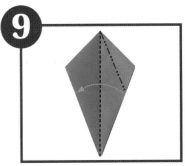

9 Squash fold on the crease formed in step 8.

10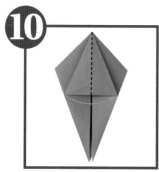

Valley fold the top flap to the right side.

11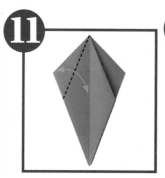

Repeat steps 8 through 10 on the left side.

12

Turn the model over.

13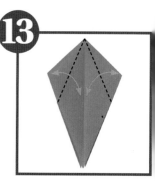

Repeat steps 8 through 11 on this side.

14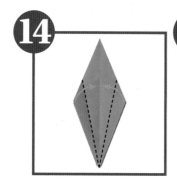

Valley fold the top flaps to the center.

15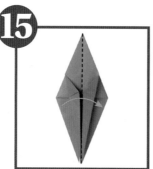

Valley fold the top two flaps to the right side.

16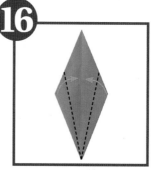

Repeat steps 14 through 15 on this side.

17

Turn the model over.

18

Repeat steps 14 through 16 on this side.

19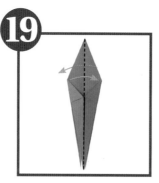

Valley fold the top flap to the right and the back flap to the left.

20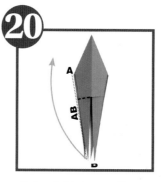

Valley fold the top flap so it lays on edge AB.

21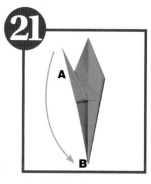

Unfold the flap.

22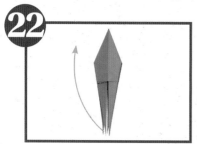

Reverse fold on the crease formed in step 20.

23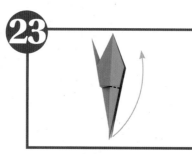

Repeat steps 20 through 22 on the top right flap.

24

Reverse fold the bottom leg almost straight out. There are no guide marks for this step.

25

Reverse fold the other leg to about the same position.

26

Valley fold the legs about ⅓ of the way from the body. There are no guides for this step.

27

Valley fold the legs at the halfway point. There are no guides for this step.

28

Unfold to step 26.

29

Reverse fold on the creases formed in step 26.

30

Reverse fold on the creases formed in step 27.

31

Unfold the bottom half of the feet.

32

Mountain fold the front legs down, starting just outside of the body.

33

Valley fold and unfold. Then gently inflate the body.

34

Mountain fold the two points to form the front feet.

35

Finished frog.

FUN FACTS

The paper crane is also a symbol of peace. In December 2004, the government of Thailand used planes to drop 100 million paper cranes over southern Thailand. The cranes were dropped in an effort to restore peace to the people fighting there.

The origins of origami can be traced back to Japan about 1,500 years ago. But the art of folding paper also developed in other parts of the world. In fact, people called the Moors introduced paper folding to the Spanish about 900 years ago.

The Secret of One Thousand Cranes Origami is the oldest known origami book. This book was published in 1797.

The longest modular origami model was a gum wrapper chain created by Gary Duschl. The chain measured more than 9 miles (14 kilometers). It used more than 1 million gum wrappers.

Every year, the American Museum of Natural History in New York City decorates an origami holiday tree. The tree stands 19 feet (5.8 meters) tall. It holds hundreds of origami models folded by members of OrigamiUSA. This organization promotes the art of paper folding in the United States.

Library of Congress Cataloging-in-Publication Data

Meinking, Mary.
 Easy Origami: A Step-by-Step Guide for Kids / by Mary Meinking and
Chris Alexander.
        p. cm.
 Includes index.
 ISBN 978-1-4296-5034-2
 1. Origami—Juvenile literature. 1. Alexander, Chris. 11. Title.

 TT870.M4243 2009
 736'.982—dc22

 2009045827

Printed in China.
102016
010091R